Paperback Quarterly

"Journal of Mass Market Paperback History"

CONTENTS

The Pecan Valley Press
Brownwood, Texas

Paperback Quarterly specializes in the history of mass-market paperbacks. Its goal is to make paperback history more comprehensive and reliable.

Paperback Quarterly features articles and notes dealing with every type (mystery, detective, science fiction, western, adventure, etc) and with every aspect of new, old and rare paperbacks.

Emphasis is placed on the historical research of paperbacks, their authors, illustrators, publishers and distributors, but the editors also invite contributions of bibliographical interest. In short, the only criterion for the editors' consideration is that the subject matter pertain to paperbacks.

Paperback Quarterly pays 1 cent per word (200-2000 words) for articles and notes. Payment on acceptance.

Paperback Quarterly is published in Spring, Summer, Fall and Winter of each year with a subscription rate of $8.00 per year or individual copies for $2.50 each. Institutional and library subscriptions are $10.00 per year. Overseas rate is $12.00. All back issues are currently out of print.

All correspondence, articles, notes, queries, ads and subscriptions should be sent to 1710 Vincent St., Brownwood, Texas 76801. (915) 643-1182.

Published and Edited by

Charlotte Laughlin   Billy C. Lee

Contributing Editors

Bill Crider   Michael Barson
Thomas Bonn   William Lyles

Printer and Technical Advisor
Martin E. Gottschalk

Cover Logo Designer
Peter Manesis

Cover Photo by Gary M. Forcier

Louis L'Amour's
Pseudonymous Works
by John D. Nesbitt

Louis L'Amour's success as the world's all-time best-selling western writer is all the more impressive when one considers that his first successful novel did not arrive until 1953 with the paperback original, *HONDO* (Gold Medal), when the author was forty-five years old. His prior publishing activities are obscure. It is reported that he received two hundred straight rejections before he sold a single word,[1] and that he authored a pseudonymous series of Hopalong Cassidy titles, but details are difficult to ascertain. Sketches of his early career usually emphasize his colorful world-wide adventures and pass over his years of anonymity, and the author himself is rather reticent about that period.

It is clear, however, that after his privately published volume of poetry, *SMOKE FROM THIS ALTAR*, appeared in 1939, he sold short stories to numerous magazines and eventually broke into the *SATURDAY EVENING POST* and *COLLIER'S* market. Some of these stories have been reprinted in *WAR PARTY* (1975) and *THE STRONG SHALL LIVE* (1980), both by Bantam.

L'Amour is particularly guarded about pseudonymous works attributed to him. He is given credit for writing some Hopalong Cassidy stories that were published in 1951 and 1952 under the *non de plume* of Tex Burns. *THE ROUNDUP*, the organ for the Western Writers of America, of which L'Amour is a long-standing member, recently stated that "Louis L'Amour wrote a long series of *HOPALONG CASSIDY* series novels, under the pseudonym of Tex Burns" (March 1980, p. 5). The *NATIONAL UNION CATALOG* lists four titles by Doubleday under L'Amour's name, with a notation to each entry that the work appeared with the pseudonym Tex Burns. *BOOKS IN PRINT* (1977-78, 1978-79, 1979-80) enters "Tex Burns, pseud." at the end of its list of L'Amour's work. Under the listing of Tex Burns one finds Aeonian Press reprints of three of the four Hopalong Cassidy Titles. *HOPALONG CASSIDY AND THE RUSTLERS OF WEST FORK, HOPALONG CASSIDY AND THE TRAIL TO SEVEN PINES,* and *HOPALONG CASSIDY: TROUBLE SHOOTER* are now in print. *HOPALONG CASSIDY AND THE RIDERS OF HIGH ROCK*, the fourth title listed in the *NATIONAL UNION CATALOG*, is yet to reappear. In contrast to these attributions,

---

[1] Hank Nuwer, "Louis L'Amour: Range Writer." References hereafter will be included parenthetically, and will refer to items (with the exception of letters cited) listed in the short bibliography that follows this discussion.

Cardboard Paperback Display Header

which imply complete authorship, L'Amour explains that he never used the name Tex Burns, but that it was the idea of a publisher who engaged L'Amour to "shape" or "tailor" some stories by Clarence Mulford, the originator of the Hopalong Cassidy stories, who was busy fishing at the time (letter from L'Amour to Nesbitt, dated 4 Feb. 1979).

Two other pseudonymous novels appeared shortly after the disputed Tex Burns novels. These works--*SHOWDOWN AT YELLOW BUTTE* (Ace D-38, 1953) and *UTAH BLAINE* (Ace D-48, 1954)--were published under the pen-name Jim Mayo.² This name may remind some readers of Crispin Mayo, the hero of L'Amour's *THE MAN FROM SKIBBEREEN*. In the early 1970's, *SHOWDOWN AT YELLOW BUTTE* and *UTAH BLAINE* reappeared under the Mayo name and then L'Amour's (*BOOKS IN PRINT*, 1971 and 1972), to join *HONDO* and other L'Amour titles under the Fawcett cover. L'Amour responds that the two Jim Mayo novels were not "unheard of for nearly twenty years" (Nesbitt, "Change of Purpose," p. 74), but that they were in print and sold well all that time (L'Amour to Nesbitt, 4 Feb. 1979). In contrast to disclaiming the Tex Burns authorship, L'Amour defends the Jim Mayo books.

While there is no evidence that the books were in print during this time (*BOOKS IN PRINT* shows no listing of these two novels until 1971, and they are not listed on the flyleaves of other L'Amour novels until the early 1970's), it is possible that the books were in circulation and sold well where paperback westerns always do—on the resale market. As an example of L'Amour's resale popularity, an article in the *SAN FRANCISCO CHRONICLE*, 22 Dec. 1975, reports that "In some prisons, according to the legend, you have to trade five other books for one L'Amour." *BOOKS IN PRINT* is not, of course, an infallible authority on the printing history, and Ace Books regrets that "the information requested is not available at this time" (letter from Jean Cascio, Marketing Assistant, to Nesbitt, 30 March 1979). But whether the books were in print, in circulation, or neither, they were not part of the regularly listed and cited canon of L'Amour's work until the early 1970's. Therefore, they have not always been recognized as part of his total production, even though they are now.

The L'Amour enthusiast, then, should be careful to distinguish between pseudonymous works attributed to Louis L'Amour (the Tex Burns novels), his actual pseudonymous works (the Jim Mayo novels), and the works published under his own name. It should also be noted that *L'Amour* is not a pseudonym, but only a variant spelling of the family name Lamoore (letter from John R. Milton to Nesbitt, 29 Jan. 1979; Walker, "Notes on the Popular Western"), just as Zane Grey's professional name was derived from his given name of Pearl Zane Gray.

---

²GUNS OF THE TIMBERLANDS appeared in a shorter magazine version under the Jim Mayo name in 1950, but it appeared as a novel in 1955 in L'Amour's name (copyright page of the 5th printing by Bantam).

The uncertain authorship of the Hopalong Cassidy books, as compared with the established authorship of the pseudonymous Jim Mayo books, leads to a reasonable conclusion. The Tex Burns novels should remain as items of incidental interest; Any studies or discussions of L'Amour's literary output should begin with the novels he lays full claim to--*HONDO* and *SHOWDOWN AT YELLOW BUTTE*, which initiated his formal novel-publishing career in 1953.

Following is a selective bibliography of secondary works citing the novels of Louis L'Amour.

Bloodworth, William A. Review of *FAIR BLOWS THE WIND. WESTERN AMERICAN LITERATURE*, 13 (Winter 1979), 365-66.

BOOKS IN PRINT, 1971, 1972, 1977-78, 1978-79, 1979-80.

Bulow, Ernest L. "Still Tall in the Saddle: Louis L'Amour's Classic Western Hero." *THE POSSIBLE SACK*, June/July 1972, pp. 1-8.

Gottschalk, Earl C., Jr. "Eggheads May Shun Novels by L'Amour; Millions Love Them." *THE WALL STREET JOURNAL*, 19 Jan. 1978, pp. 1-31.

Marsden, Michael T. "Introduction" to *HONDO*. Boston: Greeg Press, 1978, pp. v-x.

—————. "The Popular Western Novel as a Cultural Artifact," *ARIZONA AND THE WEST*, 20 (Autumn 1978), 203-14.

Milton, John R. "The Novel in the American West." *SOUTH DAKOTA REVIEW*, 2 (Autumn 1964), 56-76. Reprinted in *WESTERN WRITING*. Ed. Gerald Haslam. Albuquerque: University of New Mexico Press, 1974, pp. 69-89. See especially p. 73 in Haslam.

NATIONAL UNION CATALOG, Pre-1956 Imprints, Vol. 313, p. 378. Nesbitt, John D. "Change of Purpose in the Novels of Louis L'Amour."
John D. 'Change of Purpose in the Novels of Louis L'Amour." *WESTERN AMERICAN LITERATURE*, 13 (Spring 1978), 65-81.

—————. "A New Look at Two Popular Western Classics." *SOUTH DAKOTA REVIEW*, 18 (Spring 1980), 30-42.

Nuwer, Hank. "Louis L'Amour: Range Writer." *THE COUNTRY GENTLEMAN*, Spring 1979, pp. 99-100, 102.

—————. Review of *RIVERS WEST. WESTERN AMERICAN LITERATURE*, 11 (Summer 1976), 167.

THE ROUNDUP, Vol. 28, no. 3 (March 1980), pp. 4-5.

Seshachari, Candadai. "Popular Western Fiction as Literature of Escape." *THE POSSIBLE SACK*, April 1973, pp. 5-8.

"The Undisputed King of Paperback Westerns." *SAN FRANCISCO CHRONICLE*, 22 Jan. 1975, p. 16.

Walker, Don D. "Notes on the Popular Western." *THE POSSIBLE SACK*, Nov. 1971, pp. 11-13.

—————. "The Scholar as Mountain Man." *THE POSSIBLE SACK*, April 1973, pp. 16-17.

First Printing: Two Million
by Michael Barson

When most of us were college sophomores, we spent half our energy avoiding work and the other half looking for trouble. So who is this John Jakes, to be selling stories to pulps and having a novel published while still a DePauw undergraduate, anyway? Some people just don't know how to do anything gracefully.

Now, almost thirty years, two hundred short stories and fifty novels later, John Jakes is still plagued with success. His last novel, THE AMERICANS, enjoyed one of the largest first paperback printings ever--two million copies--and immediately settled in at the top of all the national bestseller charts. Later this year his first hardcover historical novel, NORTH AND SOUTH, will establish Jakes as a Book-of-the-Month-Club household name. But to those of us who have loved and read paperbacks for the last twenty years, John Jakes is not merely a name in our homes, but also a fixture on our bookshelves. You say you're a mystery fan? Then you must remember the four wild and witty Johnny Havoc novels he wrote for Belmont in the 1960's. Is science fiction your thing? Jakes' ON WHEELS, BLACK IN TIME, and SIX-GUN PLANET were three of the more original and provocative extrapolations of the last ten years. You prefer sword-and-sorcery? Then you know Jakes' Brak the Barbarian series, perhaps the best of the Robert E. Howard pastiches. You don't like sword-and-sorcery? Then Jakes' sendup of the genre, MENTION MY NAME IN ATLANTIS, will elicit more that a few chuckles. You're a history buff? Jakes has delved into the times and exploits of such legends as Ghengis Khan, King Richard the Lionhearted, Nero, Salome, George Washington, Teddy Roosevelt, and, of course, Philip Kent and his descendants. You say Philip Kent isn't real? Then you haven't put in enough time on Jakes' The American Bicentennial Series, the publishing success story of the 1970's for the paperback industry.

Of course, things have not always been wine and roses for John Jakes. Only seven years ago he was so depressed over having to write the CONQUEST OF THE PLANET OF THE APES novelization from the film screenplay (which netted him a princely $1500) that Jakes almost left the writing profession permanently. As a lyricist for several on- and off-Broadway shows, and a proven success in the advertising world, Jakes felt that chronicling the exploits of thrice-removed talking apes was not what he had been working towards for over twenty years. But within a year a phone call from Lyle Kenyon Engel had set Jakes on the path to bestsellerdom and financial security. Madison Avenue's loss, our gain.

In the conversation that follows, John Jakes looks back over his thirty years in the story-telling business, revealing himself to be a man whose present stardom in the publishing industry has not lessened his senses of humor and perspective. This interviewer has resolved to be just as self-deprecating and gracious when his thirty-millionth book has been sold.

Interview with John Jakes
by Michael Barson

MB: How did that series of spy stories for *The Saint Mystery Library* come about?

JJ: These were written on spec-12 short stories (later a 13th was added) featuring a spy named Roger. Whether Roger is his first name, his last name, or both, I don't know even today. The stories were spoofs, each incorporating a number in the (original) title-- one in the first story, two in the second, and so on up to twelve. Some titles were changed in publication. Hans Santesson bought the entire group as a package, publishing some in THE SAINT and some in the paperback "reader" format. A few months before Hans died, he requested copies of the stories, with an eye toward possibly editing them into an anthology. I was too poor to afford Xeroxing in those days, and (reluctantly) loaned him my file of carbons. He died, and the file disappeared. I have no copies of the stories as written, and my file of published versions is incomplete--although through the good offices of Tom Johnson, and some other pulp-and-paperback scholars, I am beginning to develop a list of the issues in which the stories were published. Obviously the next step will be to try to assemble a full set of copies of the publications--or at least Xeroxes of the stories.

MB: Was *GONZAGA'S WOMAN* your earliest novel? One doesn't hear much about it.

JJ: Now there is one I had forgotten--though my friend Jack Gaughan reminds me of it once a year or so. I am disturbed that it was never listed as copyrighted. It was my (pathetic and laughable) attempt to write a Gold Medal original paperback--in a day in which I had neither the understanding of what that meant, not the talent to do it even if I understood it. Never selling a book to Gold Medal remains one of the two biggest disappointments of my early career; the other is my inability to sell a science fiction piece to John Campbell. I did sell 6 or 8 half-hour plays to a Mutual Network science fiction radio show for which he served as host/narrator. But that wasn't the same thing; someone else bought the scripts.

MB: Michael Avallone referred to a novel you wrote in the mid-fifties for a magazine he was editing for Lyle Engel. Do you recall that?

JJ: Your question about AMERICAN AGENT magazine really brought back memories. I hadn't thought of that subject in years. Sometime in 1954-55 I did indeed write a spy novel entitled HUNTING ZERO. The Scott Meredith agency was unable to sell it until editor Mike Avallone picked it up for the first [and, I believe, only] issue of Lyle Engel's AMERICAN AGENT magazine. The novel was the featured piece, but the issue also included one of my short stories under an "Alan Payne" pseudonym which I now and then used to hide multiple contributions in a given magazine issue. My detailed records begin in 1957, so what I received for the use of the story, I can't say with certainty; my memory, which may be faulty, tells me it was $500. I do not save all my correspondence by any means. But for some curious reason, I saved a letter from Lyle Engel dated August 14, 1963, and sent to me directly, rather that care of the Meredith agency. In this letter, at which I'm now looking, Engel proposed that I consider re-working the spy novel [which Engel published under the title OPERATION ZERO] as the second book in his new Nick Carter series for Conde Nast. I recall that I did not reply [or if I did, I declined] because my arrangement with Meredith prohibited such "direct" dealings with publishers and packagers, and, more importantly, because Engel's terms were unsatisfactory: of a $500 advance, he proposed to retain two-thirds. My records, extremely accurate since 1957, show no record of any payment ever being received for additional use of this book. If indeed it became part of the Nick Carter series, this happened without my knowledge or consent, and I knew nothing of it until now. It would appear that Avallone's comment about my selling the work a second time for 'a lousy 500 bucks' is about 500 dollars too high.

MB: One of your earliest series was the "Lou Largo" one you did for Monarch in the early 1960's. Why did you choose to work under the pseudonym of William Ard?

JJ: The original proposal came from the Scott Meredith Agency. Ard had died, and someone at Monarch, maybe the editor, Charlie Heckleman, wanted to continue the Largo series that Ard had begun. The Meredith agency arranged it so that 75% of the fee went to me, and 25% to Ard's widow.

MB: Because the private eye genre is one of my favorites, I have a special place in my heart for the Johnny Havoc series you did for Belmont between 1960 and 1968. Did you enjoy writing that series as much as I think you did?

JJ: You're talking about four of my favorite books. Yes, they were very, very important to me, and I like them very much. I don't think they were very well written, but I had a ball writing them. As I recall, not one of the four emerged with its original title; Belmont, which was the only place Scott Meredith could sell these books, retitled them. Of course, they never sold well at all.

MB: Were you ever approached about licensing Havoc to either a TV or film studio?

JJ: No. But I think it would have been a knock-out as a TV-series. In fact, the actor that inspired the Johnny Havoc Character was Mickey Rooney. I was living in Ohio when I wrote the last couple Havoc books, and Mickey Rooney had come to town to Summer theater. I sent one of the Havoc books to him with a letter, hoping that he might be interested, but I never heard from him. Havoc was the champion of all the short people of the world; although I'm 6'1" I've always felt that short people, psychologically, made very strong characters. That's why Philip Kent is on the short side.

MB: Under the pseudonym Rachel Anne Payne, you wrote a gothic *GHOSTWIND* (Paperback Library, 1967). Did you enjoy working in that genre?

JJ: Yes, I did enjoy writing GHOSTWIND. I did it as a challenge, to see if I could write a novel through the viewpoint of a female character. Rachel Anne Payne, by the way, is my wife's name.

MB: As Jay Scotland you wrote a number of historical swash-bucklers. How was it that the Scotland novels appeared under both the Ace and Avon imprints? Didn't either house want to commit itself to this author's output?

JJ: The two titles that came out at Avon--I, BARBARIAN and THE VEILS OF SALOME--were done on "spec": that is, they were my own idea. The four that were done for Ace were suggested by Don Wollheim, to the point where he said (through Scott Meredith), "I would like a pirate novel," which became STRIKE THE BLACK FLAG. Neither house wanted to commit itself to Jay Scotland's output, because at the time historical novels were very difficult to sell. None of these books did well at all.

MB: Were these books researched in the same manner you researched the Kent series?

JJ: I did research each perior, but not as exhaustively as I did the backgrounds for the Kent books.

MB: With the benefit of twenty years' hindsight, how do you feel the Scotland novels hold up?

JJ: A couple of them hold up fairly well: a couple of them are absolutely wretched. ARENA was the best of the bunch. I did extensive revisions when some of these were reprinted [by Pinnacle Books, circa 1975] because I thought writing was purple prose at its worst.

Cardboard Paperback Display Header

MB: Did writing science fiction present you with any problems that, for instance, the private eye and historical formats did not?

JJ: No; Science fiction was much easier to write than the historical material, because the immense amount of research was not necessary.

MB: Do you feel you might try your hand again at writing SF?

JJ: I would like to go back and do some science fiction one of these days, but I doubt seriously that I will, strictly because the demands for my time on the historical novels are so great.

MB: You worked for several paperback houses in the early 1960's, among them Ace, Avon, Belmont and Monarch. Were there any significant differences among them in the manner they treated a writer, or conducted business in general?

JJ: No, not really. The advances were all about the same, in the $1000-$2000 range. None of the books earned royalties. Editorially I had no contact with anyone at those houses, except insofar as the Meredith Agency would occasionally send a note to me that one of the editors had written suggesting a minor change or two in a manuscript. I didn't have a favorite house, or a favorite editor, because I never got to meet any of them. Most of the work for those houses was sold on a three-chapters-and-outline basis.

MB: You have written books which were first published as hardcovers, and books which were published as paperback originals. Did you have a preference as to the form in which your work was published? Were there any advantages in contracting to produce paperback originals?

JJ: There were no advantages in producing novels for a paperback house. But it was good, dependable money, in the sense that the houses paid fairly promptly: you got a lump sum advance. I never earned any royalties on these early paperbacks. The disadvantages were two-fold: you never got any reviews (justifiably so; The work was turned out very quickly and probably didn't deserve any), and you didn't get any editorial help that might have improved the book and your overall writing. (Although I did receive some suggestions on GHOSTWIND.) To show you how much the paperback market has changed, I got fully as much editorial direction from Pyramid on the Kent Family books as any hardcover novelist.

MB: Would you discuss the manner in which Book Creations, inc. approached you to write the Kent Family series for Jove?

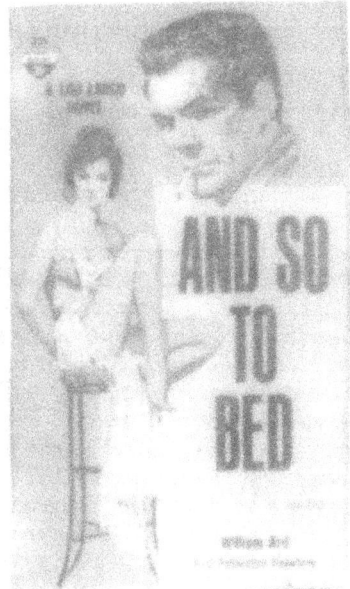

John Jakes writing as Alan Payne and William Ard

John Jakes writing as Jay Scotland

JJ: At the time the series got underway, negotiations were well along for a sale of Pyramid Books to Harcourt Brace Jovanovich. the hardcover house. HBJ wanted to go into the mass-market paperback business. They culminated the sale, took over the imprint, changed Pyramid to Jove. After a few years of trying to crack the market--and finding it difficult to do so--the imprint was sold to MCA, which also owns the Berkley imprint.

Book Creations, Inc. did not exist in 1973...Lyle Engel was a book packager--unincorporated--operating out of New York City. I received a phone call in March of 1973 from a former advertising colleague, Don Moffett. Lyle had approached him about doing this five-volume series for Pyramid Books. Don suggested that Lyle get ahold of me, since he had other commitments.

A couple of days later, Lyle called me, full of his typical enthusiasm, and described the type of series he wanted: a fictional family through American history. Really the kind of thing that Zola had done almost a hundred years earlier with his cycle of novels about the descendants of a French family. Not a new idea, but a good one, pegged to the Bicentennial.

The timetable called for five books, bringing the family up to 1976, the last book to be published not later than July 4, 1976. It was originally called "The American Bicentennial Series," and was rechristened "The Kent Family Chronicles" when it ran on beyond that date.

15

MB: When did the proposed 5-volume Kent series expand to 8? •

JJ: The need to expand the series became apparent to me about the time I finished writing THE REBELS. At that time, I still had hopes the story could be brought up to 1976 with 8 volumes. The deal for expanding the series was signed (with Pyramid) on September 10, 1975--a few weeks after publication of THE SEEKERS. Pyramid knew by then it had a hit on its hands, so was quite willing to expand to extra books. It was also about this time that I re-negotiated my terms with Lyle.

MB: How extensive was the outline, or "treatment," which Lyle Kenyon Engel developed prior to you joining the project?

JJ: He didn't provide any outline or treatment. As a condition of getting signed on to do the series, I had to provide Lyle with a relatively brief outline of how I proposed to treat all five books; and a more extensive outline for the first novel (which at that time was not called THE BASTARD). Lyle showed these treatments to Pyramid, to prove he had a writer in his stable who was willing and able to handle the assignment. Shortly after that, he revealed to me the name of the publisher (which he hadn't previously done), and after some negotiations over research money and joint copyright, I signed my agreement with him for five books.

I knew at the time, of course, that Lyle's method of operation-- keeping 50% of the earnings--was contrary to everything set forth by the Author's League, of which I was a member. Nevertheless, my career as a writer, prior to 1973, had not really gone anywhere. In fact, I was getting very depressed about it. I was making an exceptionally handsome living writing sales meetings and audio-visual presentations on a free-lance babis: I was making $150 an hour writing for clients such as RCA and General Motors.

I broke with Scott Meredith because I felt, for whatever reason, that I had been irretrievably classified as a low-on-the-scale paperback writer. The last assignment they had been able to get me was a $1500 novelization of CONQUEST OF THE PLANET OF THE APES. I felt that my career was going nowhere fast, unless perhaps it was down; That perhaps I had wasted twenty years on a false hope.

That was the frame of mind that induced me to go along with Lyle's deal, even though I knew it was contrary to all the precepts of all the writers' organizations to which I had belonged.

Lyle is a very shrewd bargainer, but I have always found him to be honest in paying what is owed. If every publisher paid as promptly as he did, writers would never have any complaint.

But after THE SEEKERS [Volume III] I went back to him and said, in effect, "Lyle, I'm very unhappy; I feel I'm contributing much more than fifty percent to these books." We then negotiated.

I came out with a substantially higher percentage of all subsequent earnings, and that arrangement is in effect now.

MB: Do you realize any additional monies if a part of the series is adapted for television, as was THE BASTARD? Or if a book club reprints your work as hardcovers?

JJ: I share in all subsidiary rights.

MB: Including *THE KENT FAMILY ENCYCLOPEDIA*?

JJ: This project was off the ground at Bantam (i.e., sold) before Jove ever knew about it--or yours truly. Unfortunately, under the terms of my original deal with Engel, while I get a good share of money from all subsidiary projects, I have no say in whether they do, or do not, get done.

I have heard--only heard--that Bantam intended to package the ENCYCLOPEDIA so that it would appear I'd written it. Some foot-stomping and teeth-gnashing by my lawyer put a stop to that.

In any case, Jove [MCA version] was quite put out that the ENCYCLOPEDIA was never offered to them. The ENCYCLOPED-IA has not done as well as other expected, and I believe this has put a stop to other projects Lyle was discussing with Bantam: the KENT FAMILY ALBUM (paintings of the characters) and (heaven help me) the KENT FAMILY COOK BOOK.

Perhaps the sincere (if that's the right word) desire of some people to actually publish such stuff will further explain my reference to some parts of publishing as suffering from 'TV mentality.' Everyone concerned (except me) was quite willing to profit from my embarrassment over these non-books. Fortunately the ENCYCLOPEDIA was pretty well written by Robert Hawkins [even if it remained largely a useless, purposeless book--as many reviewers who gave it book-review commented].

MB: Do you have any regrets about the Kent series being published as paperback originals, rather that in the more prestigious hardcover format?

JJ: No, I've never had a single regret about that. In fact, I have always believed that the series came into the market at exactly the right time, when readers were ready for major, original paperback workds. They were looking for new writers in the paperback field that they could take up, and I was lucky enough to be there in the first year of this paperback revolution. The readers created the success of Kathleen Woodiwiss, Rosemary Rogers, and yours truly.

I have never held back an ounce of energy or effort in my writing; nevertheless, I realize that I'm not a charles Dickens, or a Franz Kafka, or an Ernest Hemingway. I really think I would do very badly in the arena where the so-called critics are the arbiters.

Now that I'm doing a hardcover novel for HBJ[NORTH AND SOUTH], I'm not writing it any differently than I did the Kent series: the best I know how. I consider myself to be in the same branch of the writing fraternity as Harold Robbins and Irving Wallace: people whose favorable reviews come from the readers, rather than the academics.

If every the Kent Family series is continued, I would want it continued in paperback original format, and not have it switched to hardcovers; I think that would be disloyal to the original audience that created their popularity.

MB: You have announced that The Kent Family Chronicles will not be continued beyond Volume VIII, *THE AMERICANS.* Do you intend to return to this series sometime in the future, to take us up to the present, as you originally planned?

JJ: I've been really astonished at the volume and the emotional intensity of the mail that has come in following the conclusion of the series...I have letters from people who have stayed up all night, who have stayed up eighteen hours reading continuously...And I even have, I'm amazed to say, tearstained letters from ladies who cried as they finished the book, and immediately sat down to write a letter. A writer can ask for no more, no greater reward, than that kind of response. Perhaps, because of that, at some time in the future I could conceivably go back and pick it up again.

MB: The Kent Family Chronicles has spawned a number of similarly structured series, some from Book Creations, Inc. Do you see this trend eventually creating a glut on the market? Can the audience for paperback originals support all these series?

JJ: It's very flattering to be imitated. And it's to be anticipated that such imitations would come along from Lyle and from other pack-agers and publishers. The imitative mentality is very strong in all creative fields in this country. There are only a few original thinkers; Consequently, those who fill most of the jobs can only think, "If that was good, three more will be better." It's always more tempting to go with the proven success.

I liken hardcover publishing to motion pictures, and paperback publishing to television. The thinking I just described is more prevalent in television and in paperback publishing. One occult novel that's successful will spawn forty imitations, because it's easier and less risky. I think there's a definite danger of overkill here. Danger is too mild a word; I think it's a certainty. My hard-cover publisher, Bill Jovanovich, said to me some months ago that he felt the family-saga series concept has been beaten to death. It's his judgment that by next year the bloom will be off the rose.

MB: In five years you produced eight novels in the Kent series, which totals an incredible 5,000 pages. That seems an almost superhuman rate of production, given the extensive research that must be done for each volume. Can you discuss your working methods?

JJ: I've always been cursed--or blessed--with the ability to write very rapidly; My advertising career made that imperative. I began in the old pulp magazines, where you were paid a penny a word, so so the emphasis was on speed rather than quality. The Scott Meredith Agency really put a premium on keeping its writers working at top speed. In fact, the Meredith philosophy seemed to be, we want to get our writers signed up with eight or ten contracts, and worry later about whether they're able to produce the material on time.

I simply set myself a quota of words per day; Generally, a segment of about 2500 words. I start about 9 in the morning, and I conclude at 2 in the afternoon. Then I prepare my notes for the next day's section. I do not maintain a research staff. My wife, Rachel, helps me from time to time with specific research problems; Otherwise, I do it all myself.

MB: Can you give us the story behind that massive trade softcover that Dell put out last year, *EXCALIBUR?* How did you come to work with Gil Kane?

JJ: Gil Kane, a comic book artist, contacted me in late 1974 to provide a script for an illustrated version of the King Arthur legend. I provided a 20-25,000 word narrative with dialogue--a novelette. I sold that to him for $1000 on a buy-out basis, relinquishing all rights. What happened to it subsequently is not my work; That's all I want to say about the matter.

The Paperback Original Novels of John Jakes

General Fiction:

Gonzaga's Woman (Royal Giant #22, 1953)
G.I. Girls (Monarch, 1963)

Gothic:

Ghostwind (Paperback Library, 1967)[as Rachel Anne Payne]

Fantasy & Science Fiction:

When the Star Kings Die (Ace, 1967)
Brak the Barbarian (Ace, 1968)
The Asylum World (Paperback Library, 1969)
Brak the Barbarian vs. the Mark of the Demons (Paperback Library 1969)
Brak the Barbarian vs. the Sorceress (Paperback Library, 1969)
The Hybrid (Paperback Library, 1969)
The Last Magicians (Signet, 1969)
The Planet Wizard (Ace, 1969)
Tonight We Steal the Stars (Ace, 1969)
Black in Time (Paperback Library, 1970)
Master of Choas (Ace, 1970)
Master of the Dark Gate (Lancer, 1970)
Monte Cristo #99 (Curtis, 1970)
Six-Gun Planet (Paperback Library, 1970)
Mention My Name in Atlantis (DAW, 1972)
Witch of the Dark Gate (Lancer, 1972)
On Wheels (Warner Paperback Library, 1973)
Conquest of the Planet of the Apes (Award, 1974)

Private Eye:

This'll Slay You (ace, 1958) [as Alan Payne] "B.B. Moon"
Johnny Havoc (Belmont, 1960)
Make Mine Mavis (Monarch, 1961) [as William Ard] "Lou Largo"
And So to Bed (Monarch, 1962) [as William Ard] "Lou Largo"
Give Me This Woman (Monarch, 1962) [as William Ard] "Lou Largo"
Johnny Havoc Meets Zelda (Belmont, 1962)
Johnny Havoc and the Girl Who Had "It" (Belmont, 1963)
Making It Big (Belmont, 1968) "Johnny Havoc"

Historical:

I, Barbarian (Avon, 1959) [as Jay Scotland] (revised and reissued by Pinnacle, 1975)

The Veils of Salome (Pinnacle, 1976) [as Jay Scotland]

Strike the Black Flag (Ace, 1961) [as Jay Scotland]

Sir Scoundrel (Ace, 1962) [as Jay Scotland] (reissued as *King's Crusader,* 1977)

Arena (Ace, 1963) [as Jay Scotland]

Traitor's Legion (Ace, 1963) (reissued as *The Man From Cannae* (Pinnacle, 1977)

The Bastard (Pyramid, 1974) (Volume I of the American Bicentennial Series)

The Rebels (Pyramid, 1975) (Voume II of the A.B.S.)

The Seekers (Pyramid, 1975) (Volume III of the A.B.S.)

The Furies (Pyramid, 1976) (Volume IV of the A.B.S.)

The Titans (Pyramid/Jove, 1976) (Volume V of the A.B.S.)

The Warriors (Jove, 1977) (Volume VI of the A.B.S.)

The Lawless (Jove, 1978) (Volume VII of the Kent Family Chronicles)

The Americans (Jove, 1980) (Volume VIII of the K.F.C.)

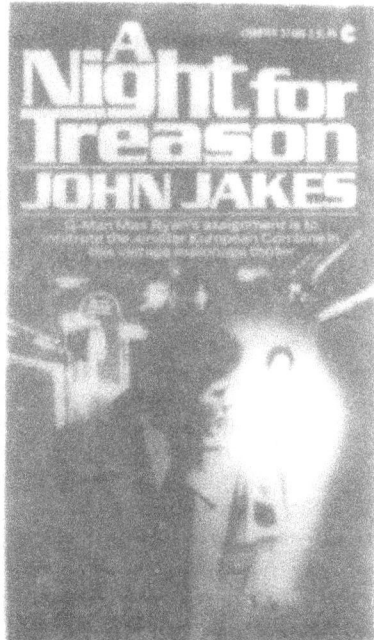

Reprints/Reprints
Ray Bradbury's FAHRENHEIT 451
by Bill Crider

The first Ray Bradbury story I ever read was "The Fireman," which I found in an old *GALAXY* magazine that someone had sold me. I was maybe sixteen years old, and I had just started reading science fiction and fantasy. I had no idea who Bradbury was and no idea about what his reputation was either in or out of the science fiction field. I just knew that I'd read a story that meant something to me, by a man who seemed to love books as much as I did. I've never forgotton it.

When "The Fireman" was expanded and published in book form by Ballantine (simultaneously in paperback and hardcover), the title was changed to *FAHRENHEIT 451*. The first paperback edition featured illustrations by Joe Mugnaini and contained two stories in addition to the title tale: "The Playground" and "And The Rock Cried Out." The front cover depicts a man (Montag?) constructed of newspaper and book pages, covering his face as he burns. The back cover features a photo of a crew-cut Bradbury staring dreamily into space.

As the book began to be reprinted, the Mugnaini cover was retained, with some variations. The background disappears, and the flames become stylized. The pile of burning books in which the burning man stands is gone. More significantly, perhaps, the two additional short stories were dropped from the book. In 1966, before the release of the movie version, a small blue box was added to the bottom right-hand corner of the cover. The box announces the movie, its stars, and its director. This edition was followed the next year with what might be considered the "true" movie tie-in. The Mugnaini drawing is replaced with a photo from the film.

Cover changes accelerated in the 1970s. The twenty-sixth printing (cover by Pepper) shows a man with stylized flames bursting from his body. Above him, books and pages are being consumed, and the Mechanical Hound appears. The "classic" edition, so labeled by the publisher, from 1973, has a different sort of cover -- flames rising from two burning books consume a half-hidden face. A 1975 edition has no flames at all; instead, a muscular man wearing no shirt is framed against a huge sun as he holds aloft a book. A pile of books is at his feet. The cover of the 1979 printing, by Barron Storey, is a much more graphic depiction of the Fireman in full uniform standing amid a huge pile of burning books and weilding his kerosene hose.

1st printing

48th printing

7th printing

16th printing

23

Kresek

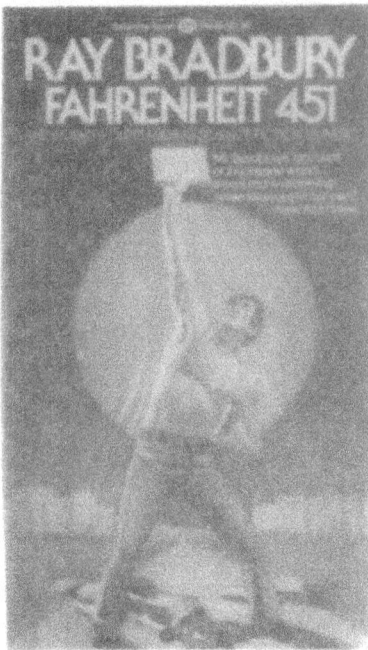

Joe Mugnaini

39th printing

3rd printing

Pepper

32nd printing

26th printing

Much more interesting than the cover changes, however, are the changes which took place in the text of *FAHRENHEIT 451* over the years. In an "Afterword" to the October 1979 edition, Bradbury writes that "some cubby-hole editors at Ballantine Books, fearful of contaminating the young, had, bit by bit, censored some 75 separate section from the novel." The hilarious irony in all this is that Bradbury's book is an attack on censorship.

The censorship began with a special "Bal-Hi" edition in 1967, an edition designed for high school students and containing an introduction by Richard H. Tyre telling parents and teachers that the issues raised by Bradbury "are exactly the issues that the morally, socially, or politically aware human being must face today." Mr. Tyre was right, but Ballantine apparently felt that students couldn't face those issues if the characters in the novel said naughty words. So on page 87 of the Bal-Hi edition two lines are dropped:

"Guy!"

"Damn it all, damn it all, damn it!"

That's one example out of 75, but it's typical of the rest. There is no mention anywhere on the Bal-Hi edition that it has been abridged, but printing histories in later Ballantine editions refer to the "Revised Bal-Hi Editions."

Unfortunately, by 1975, the deletions which had been made for the "Revised" printing began to creep into the regular editions. The thirty-ninth printing of 1975, supposedly *not* a Bal-Hi Edition, drops the same two lines quoted above from page 87. Now not only students, but all readers, would be protected from hearing Montag say damn.

Judy Lynn Del-Rey promised Bradbury that the cuts would be restored, that the book would be reset and republished. There is no indication in the printing history of the October 1979 edition that the book is a new edition, but clearly it is. The two quoted lines appear now in their proper place in the narrative, which, owing to bigger print and more white space, is on page 106. Another book has been saved from burning.

James Reasoner, a PQ subscriber, has published his first paperback original, *TEXAS WIND* (Manor Books), a private eye novel set in Fort Worth, Texas. Congratulations James.

Agatha Christie in the Dell Mapbacks
by Bill Lyles

The Tuesday Club Murders #8 (1943) [originally *The Thirteen Problems*)

The Boomerang Clue #46 (may? 1944), #664 (1953), #D340 (Feb. 1960) [originally *Why Didn't They Ask Evans?*)

Thirteen At Dinner #60 *(Sept. 1944), #770 (April 1954), #d404 (Feb. 1961)* [originally *Lord Edgware Dies*]. ·

Appointment With Death #105 (March 1946), #D236)Aug. 1958)

Murder in Mesopotamia #145 (Jan. 1947), #805 (Oct. 1954), #D405 (Feb. 1961).

Sad Cypress #172 (May 1947), #529 (1951), #D217 (Dell Great Mystery Library #12, Feb. 1958)

N Or M? #187 (1947).

The Secret of Chimneys #199 (1947), #D262 (Feb. 1959).

The Murder At The Vicarage #226 (May 1948), #888 (Feb. 1956), #R106 (Nov. 1961).

Murder In Retrospect #257 (Nov. 1948), #871 (Oct. 1955), #D384 (July 1961) [originally *Five Little Pigs*]

Cards On The Table #293 (March 1949), #912 (Aug. 1956), #R111 (Feb. 1962)

The Man In The Brown Suit #319 (July 1949), #D249 (Dec 1958).

Murder At Hazelmoor #391 (1950), #937 (Feb 1957), #R110 (Dec 1958) [originally *The Sittaford Mystery*].

Murder On The Links #454 (Nov. 1950), #D288 (May 1959).

The Labors of Hercules #491 (1951), #D305 (Aug. 1959).

Mr. Parker Pyne, Detective #550 (1951), #961 (Oct. 1957), #R109 (Feb. 1962) [originally *Parker Pyne Investigates*].

The Mysterious Mr. Quin #570 (1951), #D326 (Dec. 1959) [originally *The Passing of Mr. Quinn*].

Three Blind Mice And Other Stories #633 (1952), as *The Mousetrap* #D354 (May 1960).

without maps:

An Overdose of Death #683 (April 1953), #D370 (Jan 1960) [originally *The Patriotic Murders*].

Murder After Hours #753 (Jan. 1954), #D390 (Dec. 1960) [originally *The Outraged Heart* and *The Hollow*].

There Is A Tide #830 (1955), #D403 (Feb. 1961) [originally *Taken At The Flood*].

The Witness For The Prosecution #855 (1955), #D218 (Feb. 1958).

MURDER IN MESOPTOAMIA #145 with mapback

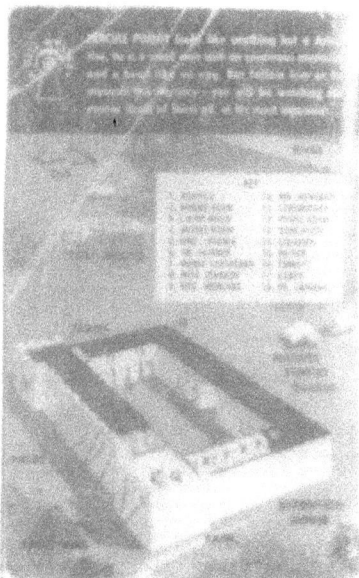

MURDER IN MESOPOTAMIA #805 with mapback

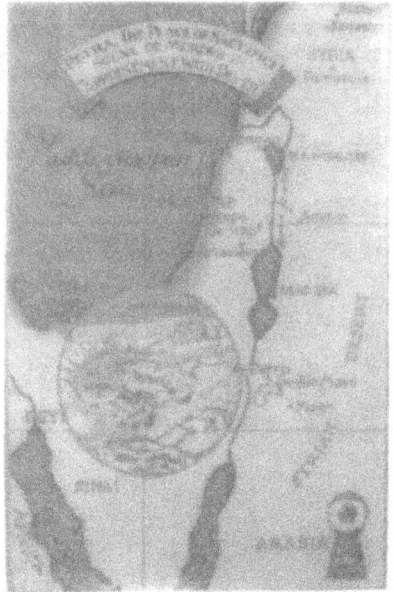

APPOINTMENT WITH DEATH #105 with mapback

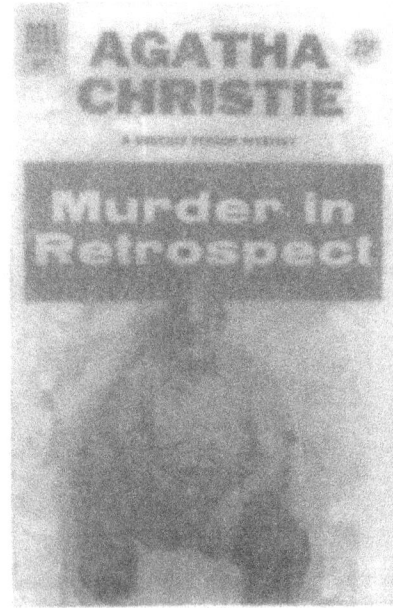

13 AT DINNER #770

MURDER IN RETROSPECT #871

A brief examination of the early Dell editions of Agatha Christie may answer a question I hear very often: How good are the Dell maps? Pretty good, I think, especially if you consider that the artists usually drew and inked the maps not from direct readings of the books but from sketchy comments made by one of the Dell editiors. (At least that is the account of on Dell editor, Don Ward, with whom I spoke a year ago.) I have not, alas, been able to track down the artists; apparently they worked separtely from the regular staff at Western Printing & Lithographing (the artists don't even remember seeing the maps). The one man who could help, the originator and editor-in-chief of Dell Books–Lloyd Smith–is long dead, and neither Western nor Mr. Smith's widow knows what happened to his papers and records.

Dell acquired early paperback rights to 22 of Agatha Christie's books, 18 of which feature maps in at least one edition; Avon and Pocket Books printed other Christie titles. (In fact, Pocket Books published THE MURDER OF ROGER ACKROYD as #5, the first U.S. mass-market paperback mystery.)

Hercule Poirot appears in 8 of the books. The first Dell Poirot is THIRTEEN AT DINNER, though in this reader's opinion not the best. The cover of #60 is colorful and provocative, deriving from pages 144 (the watch) and 236 (the pen knife or "corn knife," not much like the long needle on the cover); #770 features what I guess is Lady Edgware--I don't remember any mask in the story. And #D404 has one of William Teason's dependably smooth and stylish montages of clues from the mystery. The map of #60, of Lord Edgware's house at 17 Regent Gate, London, is beautifully drawn and quite detailed; never mind that Dame Agatha doesn't describe the house in such detail, just enjoy the map. And, as you read the book and view the scene, figure out why Mrs. Carroll can't see the woman's face.

APPOINTMENT WITH DEATH is not the best Poirot either, unfortunately. But #105 shows the genius of Gerald Gregg's airbrush, and #D236 has a striking Glaser cover, its keys a reminder of the old Dell logo. None of the details on the map of #105 is necessary, true, but some readers may not exactly have a familiarity with the area once known as Transjordan in the Near East. Too bad the map does not instead detail the layout of the camp at Petra--I find that arrangement confusing.

MURDER IN MESOPOTAMIA is fine Poirot. The cover of #145 is a bit odd (its strange evocation of eye contact appears on other Dell covers) but colorful; #805 has the standard Dell corpse (of Louise Leidner–p. 67); #D405 features yet another clever Teason montage. Both #145 and #805 have maps of the Expedition House at Tell Yarimjah (a tell is a hill), where the University of Pittsdown attempts to unearth Iraqi treasures. Both maps are based on those in the first edition and are superbly detailed–delights for the precise reader.

SAD CYPRESS may disappoint detective readers who frown at authors who don't play completely fair, but it will, I think, delight those who could care less about solutions and who prefer instead character development. The cover of #172 I'd rather forget; #529 has Robert Stanley's version of Poirot; #D217 is an attempt, in subdued Mondrian, to give dignity to a paperback. (The Mystery Writers of America gave an award to these "dignified" covers of the Dell Great Mystery Library. Give me flashy airbrushes any day.) Both maps offer slightly different views of Hunterbury Hall (in Maidensford, England);although neither seems to get the gates and roads exactly right or has the important rose trellis (p. 218), they have most everything else a careful reader might demand, even a nicely groomed kitchen garden.

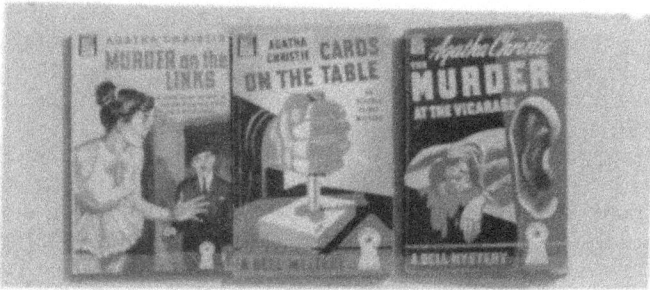

MURDER ON THE LINKS Dell#454 (cover by Al Brule)
CARDS ON THE TABLE Dell #293 (cover by Gerald Gregg)
THE MURDER AT THE VICARAGE Dell #226 (cover by George A. Frederiksen)

MURDER IN RETROSPECT, A FINE Poirot story, features strangely contrasting covers: a surrealistic view of time on #257, a dull portrait of Amyas Crale on #871 (suggesting the book as a story of a frustrated adolescent artist), and the expected, if darkish, palette of Teason on #D384. The map on #257, of the Alderbury Estate of the Crales in South Devon, like many maps in the Christie series, is well detailed and helpful--partially so because of the author's superb topographical descriptions. Maps of estates, much more difficult to design than those of houses, are unevenly done in the Dell series but usually competent on the Christie titles. This one is no exception.

CARDS ON THE TABLE is the best Poirot in the Dell series, a novel that in part parodies both Christie and her amateur detective. All covers present a symbolic penetration of cards: #293 dynamically, #912 crudely, #R111 menacingly. The map on #293 of Mr. Shaitana's Park Lane apartment in London follows what details Christie gives--fortunately, for in this book the furniture is quite important, echoing as it does the tastes of Shaitana. The map on #912 is a crude re-drawing of that on #293 (Why, I wonder, do both artists place an elevator by the entrance? No elevator is mentions in the book.)

30

CARDS ON THE TABLE #912 with mapback

THE LABORS OF HERCULES #491 with mapback

MUDER ON THE LINKS has an unfortunate cover on #454--Poirot seems to be caught peeping on a ballet dancer (explanation on p. 181). The standard Teason montage appears on #D288. The map on #454, an aerial view of Merlinville-sur-Mer, France, and surrounding area, is sumptuously done.

THE LABORS OF HERCULES delights many Christie readers. I wish I were one of them. Actually, I find the brief editorial descriptions more entertaining than the stories themselves. The cover of #491 is another Poirot vignette--here an intruder (modeled after the artist, Robert Stanley) threatens with a straight razor the just-wakened Poirot. (No hairnet?) Teason's cover for #D305 is an interesting experiment in color. The back cover of #491 presents little views of places, most of which have little to do with the book. No Blarney Castle, for example, appears in the book. The Dell maps were occasionally uninspired.

Miss Marple appears in two Dell books. *THE TUESDAY CLUB MURDERS* (#8) serves corpse on dinner plate for its front cover, and its map illustrates only one story in the book, the unexciting "Idol House of Astarte." *THE MURDER AT THE VICARAGE* presents one of the bloodiest Dell covers in #266; the other two are comparatively tame. The map on #266, of the village of St. Mary Mead (based on the first-edition map) is excellent--clear and accurate.

THE BOOMERAND CLUE, a non-series Christie, has an assortment of covers that would make the salacious American Comic Book Company drool: #46 features an immense hypodermic needle impaling a corpse (I own the original painting of of this, he boasted); #664 has a surrealistic cover that derives (very loosely, true) from page 99 (the only Dell cover by Fernando Texidor, once Dell's Art Director); #D340 indulges in bondage (see p. 184). The map on #46, of the Golf Course at Marchbolt, Wales, is attractively designed and helpful. The map of #664 is a crude re-drawing, in the pattern of Grandma Moses, with an unfortunate topographical distortion.

Tommy and Tuppence elderly clever people, are trapped by cutesiness and contrivance in *N OR M?* (#187). The cover might seem to represent important clues in the story--yet it does so imprecisely, I'm sorry to say. The map, however, of Leahampton, England, is very good; despite its large scale, it imaginatively portrays an area crucial to the novel.

The editions of *THE SECRET OF CHIMNEYS,* another non-series Christie, shows well how paperback cover art changed in 22 years: loud colors become muted, precisely and smoothly packaged letters become realistically shabby, a shadowy, gothic mansion becomes almost a blueprint in its detail. The map, cleverly drawn, accurately labeled, and beautifully colored, details "Chimneys," the county seat of Lord Caterham. The book, one of the best examples of English "good fun" detection,

THE BOOMERANG CLUE #664 with mapback

THE SECRET OF CHIMNEYS #199 with mapback

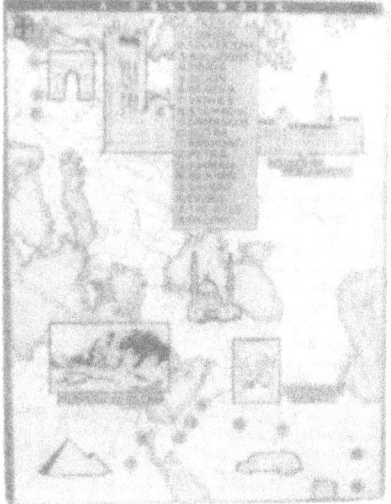

MR PARKER PYNE DETECTIVE #550 with mapback

THE MYSTERIOUS MR QUIN #570 with mapback

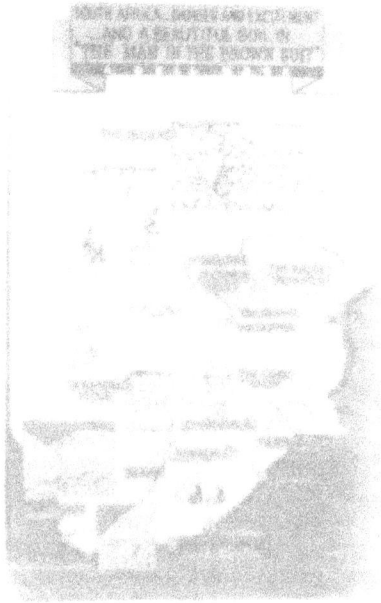

THE MAN IN THE BROWN SUIT #319 with mapback

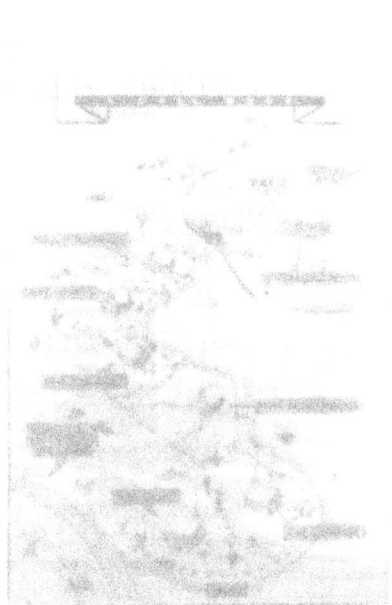

MURDER AT HAZELMOORE #391 with mapback

is full of plot twists, aliases, and delightful characters; it should appeal to any awake reader.

MR. PARKER PYNE, DETECTIVE is a collection of ambitious stories, one with the Christie-like characters, Mrs. Oliver (from *CARDS ON THE TABLE*). The cover of #550 derives from page 124 and suggests a more melodramatic book than it is. The map, ostensibly detailed, is terrible.

THE MYSTERIOUS MR. QUIN, occasionally dark stories, has an appropriately haunting cover on #570 (the only Dell cover by Robert Jonas, who did many Penguin/Signet covers), patterned after a painting mentioned in the book--"The Dead Harlequin." Teason's uncharacteristic cover on #D326 may have been inspired by pages 20-21. The map, on #570, is another series of small scenes, not all of which occur in the stories.

THE MAN IN THE BROWN SUIT, a fine early Christie non-series title, features one cover (#319) that has nothing to do with the novel; another (#D249) gives away essential clues (see pp. 26, 177; 10ff, 92ff; 30; 43ff, 177). The map on #319 does actually portray places in the story; the artist outdid himself, or herself. Interestingly, the most important inset is of the giraffe statue, so seemingly inocuous on the back cover. Read the book to see why.

MURDER AT HAZELMOOR, a bit slow-moving for Christie, pictures the important seance on the cover of #391, a section of the late Captain Trevelyan on #937, and the unimportant but dramatic-looking hurricane hamp on #R110. The map on #391 is accurate but somewhat limited in scope, only encompassing an area of Sittaford six miles from the village, in Devonshire. And the cottages should be numbered, and the road covered with snow (understandable if you read the book). The map of #907 may have snow on the road; it's hard to tell.

THREE BLIND MICE contains nine stories, four of which are connected to the map on #633. Inset #1, of 74 Culver Street (Paddington, London), and Inset #5, of Monkswell Manor (Giles and Molly Davis's boarding house in Harpleden, Berkshire--west of London), refer to the title story, dramatized so successfully as *THE MOUSETRAP.* (The acting edition of the play has a good sketch of the interior of the Manor.) Inset #2, of Waverly Court (Surrey), refers to "The Adventure of Johnny Waverly." Inset #3, of the Gallant Endeavor (a pub in the King's Road, London), refers to "Four and Twenty Blackbirds"; the artist unfortunately connects this inset to an area too far southeast of London. Inset #4m if Kaburnam Cottage (in St. Mary Mead), refers to "Tape-Measure Murder." The cover of #633 probably represents Miss Hartnell's discovery on page 98 of "Tape-Measure Murder." #D354 has--what else?--a mousetrap.

The other books have no maps, just good covers. Taken as a whole, the Dell Christies comprise a fine collection, one worth

MURDER AT HAZELMOOR #937 with mapback

THREE BLIND MICE #633 with mapback

pursuing for paperback and mystery collectors alike. Only Brett Halliday was better represented in the mapbacks, but his books hardly compare in quality to Christie's, whether the reader prefers hard-boiled fiction or little old ladies/men.

Upcoming Articles.....

Bill Lyle's article on Dashiell Hammett in Dell Mapback

Michael Barson's interview with Gil Brewer

Thomas Bonn's profile of cover artist Robert Jonas

Reprints/Reprints focus on Robert Trumbull's THE RAFT

Dell's New Mystery Line: MURDER INK and SCENE OF THE CRIME

Article on cover artist James Steranko

Thomas Bonn's profile of cover artist Lou Marchetti

Art Buchwald in Paperback

Sherlock Holmes in Paperback

Sherlock Holmes Pastiches in Paperback

Thorne Smith in Paperback

Reprints/Reprints focus on Erle Stanley Gardner's THE CASE OF THE HOWLING DOG

And Much Much More

Worth Mentioning....

Two mystery publications worthy of your support are:

MYSTERY FANcier
Guy Townsend
840 E. Main #5
Blytheville, Ark. 72315

POISON PEN
Jeff Meyerson
50 First Place
Brooklyn, N.Y. 11231

Write for details today

Soft Cover Sketches -- An Introduction
by Thomas L. Bonn

This profile of James Avati is one of four pieces I was asked to write in the Spring of 1978 by the editor of the Dutch periodical, *Utopia*. The culmination of a sabbatical leave that concerned itself with the contemporary paperback industry. The construction of these pieces forced my attention towards the design concerns of publishing softcover books and analysis of its relationship to other publishing procedures. As a result, my long-standing interest in and concern for the history and development of paperback publishing in the United States was given fresh insight by the people most directly responsible for commanding my attention when approaching a display of paperbacks.

Each illustrated during the formative years of contemporary American mass market paperback publishing, 1939-1954. Two, James Avati and Lou Marchetti, continue to paint covers today. They are recognized as being among the best in this relatively new field of commercial art.

At one time or another all four worked as salaried employees or had exclusive, long-term contracts with individual publishing houses. However, like most paperback artists, during most of their careers they worked independently in their own studios, often with assignments from two or more competing publishers on neighboring sketchbooks.

Throughout the interviews I have freely interchanged the terms "artist," "illustrator," and "painter." Whereas I recognize that out of context each term can be precisely defined, within the field of paperback publishing--and often by the cover artists themselves--the terms are freely substituted one for another.

Whatever the paperback cover artist chooses to call himself or his work, it is clear that the best of his original productions are today recognized as legitimate works of art, worthy of special exhibition, museum display, and gallery sales. The most significant tribute to these artists may only be starting to gather force. It is recognition from the growing numbers of paperback book collectors who find the combination of the traditional book format coupled with an artist's conception of its content a unique and fortuitious reflection of a society's culture.

Soft Cover Sketches --James Avati
by Thomas L. Bonn

Spring along Red Bank, New Jersey's Broad Street is accented by the pinkwhite blossoms of young cherry trees lining the block leading to James Avati's studio. This is my second meeting with the 65-year-old paperback cover artist. Unlike my first encounter six years earlier, this meeting has been difficult to arrange; our reintroduction is at first strained. Only a few weeks before someone very special to Avati had died, leaving behind ghostly images on the studio walls. Avati is generally recognized as the most respected, sensitive and durable painter in this young field.

Mention Avati's name and Bantam Books' Len Leone, undisputed capo of paperback art directors, will fantasize that should Noah ever have to take the ark out of drydock, Avati must be booked passage as publishing's cover-artist representative. Avati is special to me personally; his early artwork for New American Library first led me to recognize as a bookstore clerk that cover art added a new dimension to both the selection and reading of literature.

Avati's first commercial sketches were done for *COLLIER'S* magazine in the late 40s. In less than a year, however, he quit periodical illustration. 'I never wanted to be an illustrator, anyway. I wanted to be a painter.'

In 1949 Avati did his first paperback cover, William Gardner Smith's *THE LAST OF THE CONQUERORS*, for New American Library (Signet & Mentor Books). Soon after, Avati began to work exclusively for NAL. Unsure of himself and lacking any skilled tutor to direct his work and help him grow, Avati, somewhat to his own amazement and to the satisfaction of the publishers, developed a fresh new style for paperback covers. Avati's realistic expression of human emotion, captured from a scene in the book, for years dominated book racks and was imitated by dozens of other young cover artists. But early success took its toll.

I had to fight for most of my ideas; I had to fight grimly. The reason was that that was my only stock-in-trade. If I couldn't do what I did, I couldn't do anything... I was trying to learn how to be an illustrator out of necessity, how to be an artist because I didn't have any training. So it was a rather desperate thing for me, and my concern was always the failure I was sensing in my mind. At the same time, the publisher was falling over himself, congratulating me because whatever I was doing I was doing very well. Now you

Cover Art by James Avati

Cover Art by James Avati

Cover Art by James Avati

have to put it in context. I was a time when most of the cover art being used·was not very good; my competition wasn't very great. But as I look back at the covers -- the ones that I felt excitement about -- I still respect those covers, maybe a tenth of what I did for those people at that time. I think somehow or other they managed to combine things, not out of sophistication, but out of my own naivete and, if you will, desperation.

By the mid-50s, the 'Avati look' no longer sold books. This followed some bad art direction -- 'A publisher's first instinct is to imitate what has been saleable' -- and agonizing experiments at adjusting and tightening his compositions. 'I came up with another style, a paper-thin style.'

Avati was rescued by the sympathetic hand of Len Leone, then newly-appointed art director of Bantam Books. Avati learned how to be guided by someone he could respect, someone who understood what he, as an artist, was going through. 'I got into another school of thinking altogether,' Avati remembers, 'under an art director who fed me ideas and aesthetic direction.'

Avati reads every book he is asked to illustrate. Yet for Leone, 'I didn't have to read the book. He worked it all out for you. He scribbled this wonderful controlled shape. It always had an intriguing message.'

Today Avati works exclusively for another art director, and another publisher, Pocket Books. A contract with a publisher provides a cover artist with security by guaranteeing a certain number of cover assignments per year; for the publisher it means, among other things, that the artist cannot be used by the competition. Most paperback publishing companies have one or more artists under contract.

How does he put a cover together today? Avati summarizes it poignantly:

I read the book and put it aside and go to bed. I'll think of all the possibilities and cancel some out because they are not saleable of may have a negative appeal. I'll have a few, maybe only one left. I'll call up the art director and the thing will jell. Maybe I'll make up some little scribbles. We'll settle it over the phone, or maybe I'll go up and visit. No time is wasted. I couldn't go through elaborate discussions (such as they have at cover conferences in most publishing houses). I couldn't; the threat is too tenuous.

With more than touch of regret, Avati observes that today's covers are a lot of noise. Many covers are conglomerates of things suggesting a lot of pace inside the story; but, when it comes right to it, they are rather shallow symbols. And the stories themselves are rather shallow, too.'

Avati further reasons, 'When a really good book comes along, the problem is how to get people to read it with so much exaggerated hyperbole about. Nobody is going to believe you, not your copy, not your design, not your artwork.' Because it is hard to say anything that means anything on a cover, an artist finds himself misleading his audience by putting on the cover something other than what is really inside.

The Avati solution is a reflection of his early artwork, 'I believe that the one way left is to be honest. Everyone else is being phony. But then, you don't have to put on any cover at all.'

Quotable Quotes

Many forces have altered the shape of the book industry during the past decade. None has been more powerful than the development of paperback books and their channels of distribution. The use of the phrase "paperback revolution" has not been unjustified.

Publishers Weekly
January 1960

Collecting Original
Paperback Cover Art
by Robert Weinberg

As both a collector and dealer in original cover-art used for paperbacks (as well as science-fiction magazines and pulps) I AM OFTEN ASKED "Why bother?" The art is hard-to-find, rarely cheap, and difficult to store if not on display. I can answer this question in one of two ways.

As a dealer, the reply is quite simple. "Value." In the past few years, collecting paperbacks has become a legitimate hobby with new collectors constantly joining the market. The interest in original artwork has also mounted steadily. Originals which sold for a hundred dollars or less only five years ago are now selling for three and four times that price--and in some rare instances, ten or twenty times that price. With large private collections, art galleries and museums all showing signs of interest in popular culture, it seems logical to assume that the prices of paperback original artwork will continue to soar in the next few years. I have no doubts that in a few years, collectors will look back on this period as the "Golden Age" for obtaining originals. Prices may seem high now, but in a few years, they will appear dirt cheap in retrospect. Paperback art is a superior investment when compared to some of the prices already being asked by paperback dealers for scarce paperbacks. I have sold a number of Ace paperback paintings for prices comparable to what some of the higher-priced dealers have been asking for just two or three collectible books!

There are a number of reasons to collect original art purely from the viewpoint of a collector. For one, the low price of artwork makes it more and more attractive when compared to some of the silly prices being asked for the books themselves. Moreover, the paintings are *unique*; they are one of a kind items. Even the rarest paperback is probably in several collections. It is just one of thousands of identical copies produced. The cover art is an original piece of work and is the only one of its kind. An original makes the owner's collection unique. No matter what another collector might own, he does not possess the paintings in your collection--setting your collection apart from any other.

Third, and most important, the art itself is often stunning and is always much better than the reproduction used on the actual cover. The color presses used to print paperback covers rarely catch the color or subtle shadings or the originals. The difference between the originals and the reproductions is day and night. Often one does not even resemble another. Art editors

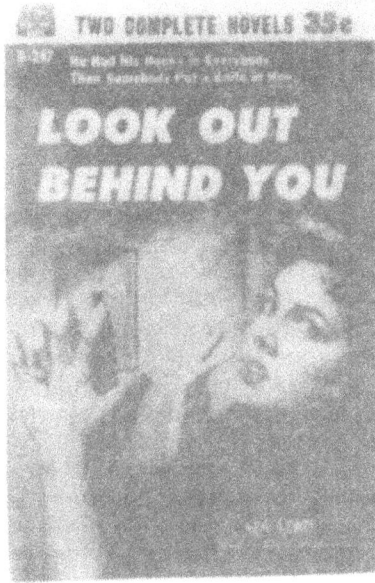

Original Painting and Paperback Cover

Original Painting and Paperback Cover

often crop large parts of the paintings from the cover, cover much of the painting with garish lettering, and even change the coloring used by the artist. Look at your favorite paperback cover; mentally remove all of the lettering, the price, the dark shading. Brighten the picture and the clarity ten times, and you might have some idea of what the original looks like. If that is not enough of a reason to collect original paperback art, then the field is not for you!

Collecting original art also is satisfying for other reasons. In the late 1950's, my favorite fantasy novel was *SWORD OF RHIANNON* by Leigh Brackett, one side of the Ace Double Book D-36. I later met and became good friends with Leigh and her husband Edmond Hamilton. So, it was an unexpected thrill when I obtained the cover painting for this book. Not only is it a masterful painting by Schultz, but it has attachments far beyond that of a mere painting. I've heard similar sentiments expressed by a collector of the works of Phillip Jose Farmer who had just bought a painting done for one of Farmer's novels. More than any first edition, these paintings are true collectors items.

Finding original artwork is a challenge. It is not easy, but it is no more difficult than obtaining anything rare. I am not revealing any professional secrets when I state the best way to buy originals is from the artists themselves. To many of these artists, painting is (or was) a way to earn a living. They do note have any great affection for their work and often are willing to sell it to the collector at a reasonable price. In many cases, on older works, the paintings might be buried in an attic and gathering dust. Unfortunately but true, I have contacted a number of artists who have burned or given away much of their originals because they took up so much room.

A number of publishers did not return original cover paintings in the past (Now, except in rare cases, artwork is always returned to the artist). In most cases, the publishers either destroyed the paintings or have them stored away in a warehouse and forgotten. Getting them to release such stored artwork is next-to-impossible. However, a few years ago, Ace Books did clear out such a warehouse and nearly 750 paintings dating back to some of their earliest paperbacks, were made available to art dealers. While many of these paintings have been sold to collectors, a good number of them are still in circulation or can be found in the stock of the small but growning number of dealers specializing in paperback cover art.

Science Fiction cover paintings also turn up quite often at Science Fiction conventions and from SF dealers. SF fandom has always been collecting oriented and fans contacted artists for magazines and paperbacks during the past fifty years. Many originals were bought and still remain in the field. Lastly, but most importantly, originals turn up from the oddest sources once

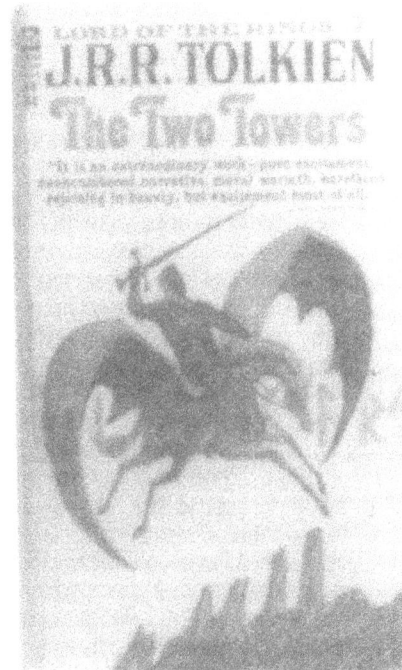

Original Painting and Paperback Cover

Original Painting and Paperback Cover

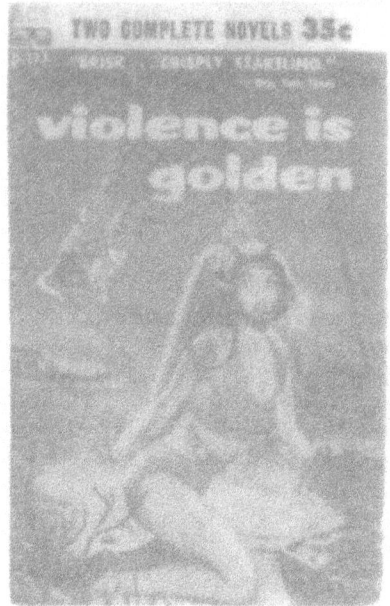

Original Painting and Paperback Cover

it is known you are looking for them. I have been offered paintings from antique dealers, from authors who bought them from the artist and then tired of the art years later, and from other collectors. As is often the case in any field, I've traded for paintings as well.

Ater buying a painting, the collector should clean, mat, and fram the art—unless it has already been cleaned by the seller. If the painting is old and in bad condition, it might pay to have it restored--that is find someone who can clean it, fix any tears or rips, and perhaps even do any minor repaintings of scratches or rubbed spots. A good cleaning and an attractive frame will multiply the beauty of any painting many times and is always well worth the price.

As to advice to a beginning collector, there are several important rules to follow. First, and most important, is to collect what you like. You have to live with what you buy--if you purchase a painting just to buy something and it is not something you like, then entire purpose of collecting it is gone. Secondly, buy what you can afford. Work by Boris Vallejo and Michael Whelan are among the best art being done in paperbacks today, but they also range from $2000-$4000 each. If you can afford these prices and want that work, go to it. Otherwise, start with more modest aims.

48

Lastly, and a good rule to follow in collecting anything, is to study the field and try to learn everything about it you can. The more you know, the better chance you will have to find a bargain- or at least to recognize it when one comes along. The easiest way to make sure you don't overpay or get cheated in a transaction is to know what you are doing. Knowledge is everything. The more you know, the easier and more fun collecting will be. It is an exciting field, one that is still just in its early stages, and there are bargains to be found. Now is the time to find them. Good luck and go to it!

In an effort to keep our readers better informed of mass market paperback history, the editors of PQ are asking all readers to clip or photo copy all newspaper, magazine, and fanzine articles that deal with mass market paperback books, authors, publishers and distributors excluding COLLECTING PAPERBACKS?, MEGAVORE, and PUBLISHERS WEEKLY. We would also appreciate hearing about newly published reference books that deal with mass market paperbacks. Your support is appreciated.

The Editors

Bunker Books
P.O. Box 1638
Spring Valley, CA 92077

WANTED TO BUY: ALL AVON PAPERBACKS, BUT ES-
PECIALLY THE FOLLOWING:

27 Avon Book of Puzzles
38 Chandler   THE BIG SLEEP
63 Chandler   FIVE MURDERERS
65 Hershfield   NOW I'LL TELL ONE
86 Avon Mystery Story Teller
88 Chandler   FIVE SINISTER CHARACTERS
90 Avon Ghost Reader
96 Woolrich   BLACK ANGEL
101 Avon Improved Cook Book
104 Irish   IF I SHOULD DIE BEFORE I WAKE
110 Terror At Night
127 Eastern Shame Girl
133 Naughty 90's Joke Book
136 Lovecraft   THE LURKING FEAR
162 Avon Book of Crosswords-Cryptograms
184 Girl With The Hungry Eyes
214 Merritt   FOX WOMAN
219 Chandler   FINGERMAN
220 Irish   I MARRIED A DEAD MAN
264 Nebel   SIX DEADLY DAMES
277   Lewis   PERELANDRA
281 Coblentz   INTO PLUTONIUM DEPTHS
285 Farley   EARTHMAN OF VENUS
295 Adams   Avon Book Of Puzzles
298 Swados   HOUSE OF FURY
308 France   MUSH, HASHISH AND BLOOD
314 Vechen   NIGGER HEAVEN
339 Kennerly   TERROR OF THE LEOPARD MEN

Top dollar paid. The better the condition, the more I will pay.
I also will trade for them, using paperbacks, digests, and
pulps from my extensive stock. I also need a copy of A1
Bantam (Rex Stout) THE RED THREADS! I will pay or trade
high.

Letters

To the Editor:

The interesting article by Mark Schaffer, "Interior Paperback Art" in the Summer issue, is illustrated with rather hazy reproductions of, among other things, Bantam endpapers. Most of those are credited, not all of them correctly.

The group of artists that worked for Bantam around that time (1945 and 1946) nearly all knew each other. They were recruited by Bantam art director Gobin Stair, who had previously helped with the production and design of Penguin Books. When Ian Ballantine left Penguin to found Bantam Books, Stair went along. It was Gobin Stair who designed the handsome format for the early Bantams. In a recent letter to me, he wrote, "The cover and endpaper plans were to emphasis the book quality, and I worked out the identifying format, which came from the three-piece binding designs used in cloth cover cases, and the prominence of the trademark." Robert Foster, incidentally, drew the Bantam "rooster."

Stair picked the cover artists from "the successful craftsmen working in the book publishing business who were sensitive to literature and to good book design and also knew what was going on in the art world and were not overpowered by advertizing dogma" (same letter). Some of these artists Stair already employed during his Penguin years: David Triggs, Lester Kohs and Edgard Cirlin. One should especially recognize the very proflific H. Lawrence Hoffman (misspelled "Zoffman" in *PQ*, twice!).

Hoffman had, in the early forties, a design studio together with freelance book designer Sol Immerman. Together, they produced book covers for Pocket Books, Popular Library (almost all books of the first years) and Bantam Books. "IM-HO" was their joint signature; "Hoffman" was Hoffman's. Hoffman did some Penguin covers for Stair, and for Bantam he did the first title, "Life on the Mississippi." He continued to do covers for Bantam for some years, including some marvellous endpapers.

Another important Bantam endpaper artist was Rafael D. Palacious, who still works as a calligrapher and cartographer now. He, and Edgard Cirlin, Ava Morgan (Weiss) and Riki Levinson shared a studio at the time those Bantam covers were produced.

Lester Kohs also did some interesting Bantam covers; I STRONGLY SUSPECT THAT HE MADE THOSE STRANGE PHOTOGRAPHIC—COLLAGE COVERS ("Was It Murder?" among them), which, although unsigned, seem to come from the same artistic hand. The (partly photographic) cover of "Old Lover's Ghost" (Bantam 114), in any case, is signed by Kohs. (Does anybody have an opinion on this?)

51

Bill English was mainly a hardcover artist but he did some wonderfully imaginative designs for Bantam endpapers and covers. His endpaper map for "First Come, First Kill" (page 47 in *PQ*) is better than most Dell "mapbacks"!

The above information is to be found in "Paperbacks U.S.A.: A Graphic History, 1939-1959" by undersigned, a Dutch edition of which will be on the market by January 20th.

Piet Schreuders
Balistraat 30 huis
1094 JM Amsterdam
The Netherlands

(continued from page 54)
cover sketch of the lady in denims and checked shirt seated at her typewriter. The novelist of course is Grace Metalious, author of *PEYTON PLACE*. The back cover of *PEYTON PLACE* features a photo of Grace Metalious and you guessed it, she's wearing denims and checked shirt and is seated at her typewriter. Mr. Packer's story, however, adds a new note. The novelist in Packer's book is poisoned by an overdose of an aphrodisiac!

NAL First -- New American Library's first paperback original was *KISS OF DEATH* (Penguin #642) by Eleazar Lipsky. As the cover indicates in the top right-hand corner, Lipsky's book was made into a movie by Twentieth Century-Fox starring Brian Donlevy, Victor Mature, and Coleen Gray. Scenes from the film are featured on the inside of both the front and back covers. The front cover was painted by Robert Jonas. Watch for Thomas Bonn's profile of Robert Jonas in the next issue of *PQ*. NAL's second paperback original was Horace McCoy's *NO POCKETS IN A SHROUD*.

An Almost -- Berkley Books was almost Merit Books! When Berkley began its paperback line in 1955 they planned to call their line Merit Books. But When Berkley learned that the name "Merit" was used for a brief time by a Chicago based publisher several years earlier, they decided to use the name "Berkley." Charles R. Byrne was Berkley's first editor.

American Paperback Cover Art Exhibition

From January 20th to March 7th of 1981, the First International American Paperback Cover Art Exhibit will be held at Gemeentemusem, The Hague, Holland. The exhibit will focus on the art and disign of American paperbacks and their covers. There will be over 1500 paperback books on display arranged three different ways: chronologically, by publisher, and by artist. There will be numerous original art on display as well.

Accompanying the exhibit, a 250-300 page catelogue/book entitled **PAPERBACKS, U.S.A.: A GRAPHIC HISTORY, 1939-1959** will be published. The catalogue will have 32 pages of color illustrations and many black & white reproductions. The first part of the catelogue will consist of a short history of European paperbacks and American paperbacks in the 19th and 20th century. The second part will focus entirely on the cover art: the general development of cover styles, different artists in different periods, recurring themes, movie tie-ins, dust jackets, redrawn covers, the function of art directors, artistic influences, recognition of cover art, and some remarks from artists themselves. the third part will consist of various appendices, a year-by-year account from 1939-1959, a register of paperback publishers, and an illustrated register of paperback cover artists.

Piet E. Schreuders, a free-lance disigner and publisher of two magazines, will be editor of the catelogue. For more details on the exhibit and the availability of **PAPERBACKS, U.S.A.**, write to Piet E. Schreuders, Balistraat 30 huis, 1094 JM AMSTERDAM,The Netherlands.

Spotlight

Every paperback has a story of its own which makes it a unique part of mass market paperback history. The story may involve the cover illustrator, the author, the publisher, or the distributor, but there is a story to be told about every book -- our job is to uncover that story.

PEYTON PLACE Take-Off -- At first glance, *THE GIRL ON THE BEST SELLER LIST* (Gold Medal, 1960) by Vin Packer is just another Gold Medal original. The plot concerns a girl who writes a sensational expose of the seamy side of life in her home town and thereby incurs the wrath of her neighbors. Up to this point the parallel with one of the better publicized female novelists of the late 1950s is pretty apparent. Gold Medal has even used a

(continued page 52)

fantasy newsletter

The Monthly News Magazine
of the Fantasy & Science Fiction Field

With the mushrooming of the Science Fiction/Fantasy field over the last few years, it has become increasingly difficult to keep abreast with the Science Fiction/Fantasy scene. One magazine which has succeeded is FANTASY NEWSLETTER.

Displaying one of the most professional layouts of any magazine in this genre, FANTASY NEWSLETTER takes its subscribers each month on a personal tour to meet the books and the bookmen;the trade and the mass-market; the fan press and the New York publisher; the authors and the illustrators. From Science Fiction/Fantasy movies to Specialty Publishers to indept interviews with your favorite authors, FANTASY NEWSLETTER puts it all together, packaged in its own original cover art.

FANTASY NEWSLETTER provides total coverage with sections like....

The Outlook, Specialty Publisher's, Trade Books, Mass-market Paperbacks, Fan Press, On Fantasy with Karl Edward Wagner/ Fritz Leiber, *Editorials, Book Reviews, Interviews, and Science Fiction/Fantasy Convention coverage.*

Remenber, for comprehensive Science Fiction/Fantasy coverage turn to the Monthly News Magazine of the Fantasy & Science Fiction Field, **FANTASY NEWSLETTER.**

For only $12.00 you will recieve 12 generously illustrated issues keeping you informed of the total Science Fiction/Fantasy scene. All copies are mailed in a sturdy envelope. Send all correspondence, queries, and subscriptions to Paul C. Allen, 1015 West 36th St. Loveland, Colorado 80537.

Subscribe Today!

★ ★

Book Sellers

The following people sell paperbacks. Most mail out booklists on a regular basis and all are knowledgeable paperback bibliophiles. For specific wants write directly to the addresses below and please include S.A.S.E.

BILL & PAT LYLES
77 High St.
Greenfield, MA 01301
(413) 774-2432

SCOTT OWEN
P.O. BOX 343
Moraga, CA 94556

GRAVESEND BOOKS
Box 235
Poconopines, PA 18350

KEITH EKBLAW
1908 D George Washington Way
Richland, Washington 99352

JUDY K. REYNOLDS
9969 B Sloanes Sq.
St. Louis, MO 63134
(314) 429-6654

JEFF MEYERSON
50 First Place
Brooklyn, N.Y. 11231

JACK IRWIN
16 Gloucester Lane
Trenton, N.J. 11231

FANTASY ARCHIVES
71 Eight Ave.
New York, N.Y. 10014

BILL LIPPINCOTT
Dunbar Hill Rd.
North Anson, ME 04958

MICHAEL BARSON
117 Crosby St.
Haverhill, MA 01830

JAN LANDAU
Rt 2 Box 293
New Castle, Virginia 24127

FAMILY PAPERBACKS
4016 Central Ave. N.E.
Minneapolis, MN 55412

BILL LOESER
P.O. BOX 1702
New Bern, NC 28560

THE ODYSSEY SHOP
1743 S. Union Ave.
Alliance, OH 44601

ED KALB
3227 E. Enid Ave.
Mesa, Arizona 85204
(602) 830-1855

JEFF PATTON
3621 Carolina St., N.W.
Massillon, OH 44646

McCLINTOCK BOOKS
P.O. Box 3111
Warren, OH 44485

FANTASTIC WORLDS BOOKSTORE
4816 A Camp Bowie Blvd.
Fort Worth, Texas 76107

BUNKER BOOKS
P.O. BOX 1638
Spring Valley, CA 92077
(714) 469-3296

PAPERBACK PARADISE
468 Centre St.
Jamaica Plain, MA 02130

BARRY & WALLY PATTENGIL
Rt 3 Box 508
Waco, Texas 76708

THE OLD BOOK STORE
210 E. Cuyahoga Falls Ave.
Akron, OH 44310

MURDER BY THE BOOK
194 ½ Atwells Ave.
Providence, RI 02903

GALE SEBERT
Sebert's Books
Leivasy, WV 26676

LUCILE COLEMAN
P.O. BOX 610813
North Miami, FL 33161

PANDORA'S BOOKS LTD
Box 86
Neche, ND 58265

MOSTLY MYSTERIES BOOKS
398 St. Clair Avenue East
Toronto, Ontario M4T 1P5

If you are a bookseller and would like you name and address printed in "Book Sellers," please drop us a line. Please tell us if you sell paperbacks by mail and/or have a retail store. We are also interested if you mail out lists on a regular basis. Happy Paperback Hunting!

www.ingramcontent.com/pod-product-compliance
Lightning Source LLC
Chambersburg PA
CBHW021225020426
42331CB00003B/477